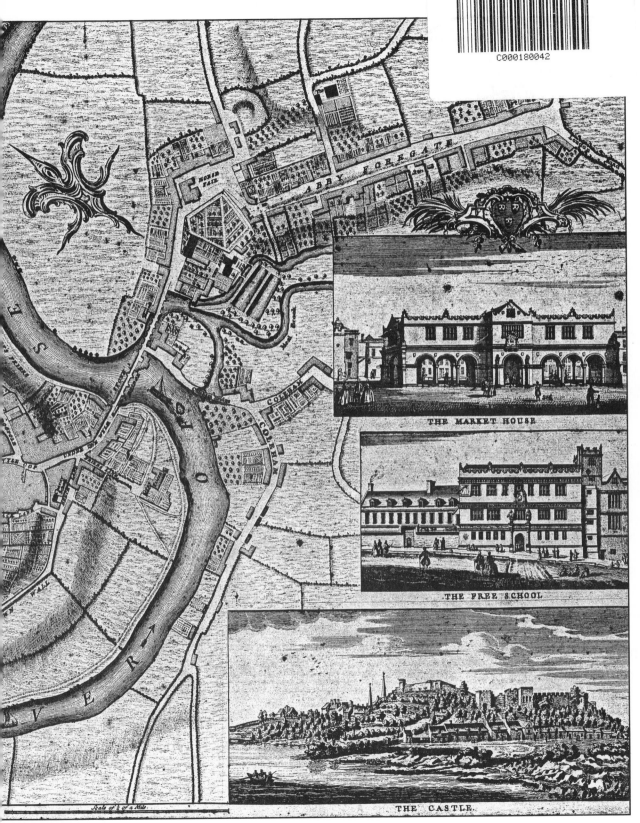

John Rocque's map of Shrewsbury, 1746.

SHREWSBURY
A Pictorial History

John Brown

Bought in Shrewsbury
14th March 1995

—

Mardol Head in December 1890. The scene typifies the character of Shrewsbury as a county town. A farmer in an old-fashioned top hat and smock passes the time of day with a town acquaintance.

SHREWSBURY
A Pictorial History

FISH STREET IN MARCH 1995 — PHOTO JOHN BROWN

Tony Carr

Phillimore

1994

Published by
PHILLIMORE & CO. LTD.
Shopwyke Manor Barn, Chichester, Sussex
in association with
Shropshire County Council

ISBN 0 85033 933 2

Printed and bound in Great Britain by
BIDDLES LTD.
Guildford, Surrey

List of Illustrations

Frontispiece: Mardol Head, 1890

Acknowledgements

The frontispiece, illustrations 130 and 159 were photographed by Samuel Butler, the author of *The Way of All Flesh*, who knew Shrewsbury well; they are reproduced by permission of the Master and Fellows of St John's College, Cambridge. Illustrations 15 and 101 are © RCHME Crown copyright and are reproduced with kind permission from the National Buildings Record.

All other illustrations are taken from the rich collections of the Shropshire Records and Research Unit. The existence of these collections is due to the kindness of members of the public who have given material, to local societies and newspapers who have transferred their own photographic records and to the efforts of library staff to preserve visual records, often in difficult physical and financial circumstances, over the past century.

Introduction

Shrewsbury first attracted the attention of artists around the year 1700. The earliest pictures are in the form of panoramas from vantage points around the town. These views record a lively, imposing, attractive, commercial centre which was also becoming the fashionable resort of the local gentry from a wide area. For these people, many with grand but isolated country estates, Shrewsbury was the natural place to congregate to meet their peers. This is the dashing Shrewsbury of Farquhar's play *The Recruiting Officer*, written in 1706 and set in the *Raven Inn* in Castle Street. Visiting the town in 1698, Celia Fiennes noted that 'there are abundance of people of quality lives in Shrewsbury more than in any town except Nottingham; its true there are noe fine houses but there are many large old houses that are convenient and stately, and it is a pleasant town to live in and great plenty which makes it cheap living.'

Soon there were to be several new fine houses as local families built town houses in which to live during part of the year. These handsome 18th-century brick buildings are to be found throughout the town, but they are particularly prolific in the streets south of Old St Chad's church. Many were newly-built for particular families, such as Broom Hall built for the Kynastons in the 1730s and Abbey House built *c.*1700 for the Jenkins family, which contains a staircase with a wide landing, designed, it is said, to allow a sedan chair to be turned with ease. Some, in fact, are only superficially Georgian; these deceivers, the Old House in Dogpole, Clive House and the former Liberal Club in Belmont, for example, are really much older timber-framed buildings with brick veneers designed to make them seem more modern. Others had their distinctive timber-framing plastered over in an attempt to conceal their true origins in less gracious times; there are still some Shrewsbury buildings that retain these plaster disguises though a few of them also have, rather confusingly, the illusion of timber-framing painted on the plaster. The conversion, late in the century, of the Castle to provide a desirable residence for the wealthy Shrewsbury M.P. Sir William Pulteney first brought the Scot Thomas Telford to the county, a move which had far-reaching effects on Shropshire. The house he created has largely disappeared, but the one surviving room and the summer house on the castle mound provide hints of its former Gothick elegance.

Besides the many imposing houses, a number of public buildings, many of them charitable institutions, were built in the town in the 18th century. Bowdler's Charity School in Beeches Lane dates from 1724. In Frankwell, the handsome buildings of Millington's Hospital and School are little changed since their construction in 1749. The Public Subscription School, started in 1708, moved to new premises at the east end of the English Bridge in 1779. Almost unrecognisable under its late 19th-century re-working is the impressive Foundling Hospital building of 1760-5 now part of Shrewsbury School; this was built by the London Foundling Hospital for £12,000 to receive some of its metropolitan orphans but the experiment proved too costly to maintain and it closed in 1774. The building was soon put to a new use when it became the town's workhouse under the name the House of Industry; this was in 1784, but fifty years later it was described as 'a complete failure' as it received only a small number of the town's poor due to mismanagement.

Perhaps the most important 18th-century philanthropic introduction was the Infirmary, which was established in 1745 in the unfinished Kynaston house called Broom Hall by St Mary's church. For most of its long history on this site, the Salop Infirmary was financed directly by public subscriptions administered by leading county families acting as Trustees. In exchange for annual donations, monied families in Shropshire and further afield could have their servants, tenants or acquaintances treated in the Infirmary, they themselves, of course, being attended by medical men at home. A number of Society events became associated with fund-raising for the Infirmary, the most important being Hospital Sunday at St Chad's church. This was attended by the whole of fashionable society in town to enjoy the races and other amusements such as balls; the collection was added to the Infirmary's funds. Broom Hall had to be extended by two additional wings in 1787 to cope with the increased demands made on the hospital which was one of the most valued County institutions.

For differing reasons, three of Shrewsbury's five ancient parish churches were rebuilt in the 18th century. St Julian's church was rebuilt in 1749-50 to the design of the local architect Thomas Farnolls Pritchard; the old building was said to be ruinous. In 1788, St Chad's church actually became a ruin when part of the tower dramatically collapsed, bringing with it most of the north side of the ancient building; the decision to rebuild on a new site close to the elegant new houses on Claremont resulted in an unusual round church, opinion of which has been divided since its difficult birth in committee to the present day. Alarmed by the collapse of St Chad's, those responsible for St Alkmund's church obtained an Act of Parliament to demolish their medieval building before it too fell down; some contemporaries considered this unnecessary and gleefully recorded that not only did the old building need blowing up with gunpowder, such was its soundness, but that its replacement quickly proved to be poorly-built and in need of constant expensive maintenance. The new St Alkmund's was in fact a handsome Georgian Gothick preaching room which has been ruined by late 19th-century alterations. Protestant Nonconformity was long established and strongly supported in Shrewsbury. However, the Presbyterian chapel in the High Street had to be rebuilt after its destruction by an anti-Government mob in 1715. A schismatic section of this congregation set up their own chapel on Swan Hill in 1767 and the Baptists, Quakers and Roman Catholics had their own chapels by 1800. There was evidently fierce rivalry for support and status between the various forms of worship which, to some degree, could be affected by the modernity of the place of worship hence the enthusiasm for church and chapel building in this century.

Other buildings or places where fashionable society gathered were introduced or modernised in the 18th century. The Quarry was planted with lime avenues in 1719, an early example of municipal provision of a public park. A theatre was built within the remains of a 14th-century stone mansion in Shoplatch and attracted a wide variety of national and regional theatrical companies including the great Sarah Siddons. The room over the Market Hall was used by John Weaver, a native of Shrewsbury who also worked in the London theatres, to house a performance of 'scenical dancing', or as we should now call it ballet, a form of theatre he did much to reintroduce. The Shirehall was built in the Square to house town and county administrative business and to provide law courts; its Green Room was also used for balls and other social gatherings until the construction of the impressive Assembly Room at the *Lion Hotel*, *c.*1777. The scale and magnificence of this room, which retains its period details, are a powerful reminder of the pre-eminent social position held by the town in the Georgian period. Due to the work of the numerous turnpike road trusts, road communications improved considerably during the latter half of the 18th century; several Shrewsbury inns, the *Lion*, the *Raven* and the *Talbot* for example, were rebuilt to encourage coach travellers to stay for a few days to see the attractions of the area. A town history was published in 1779 followed by visitors' guides in the 1780s to inform the traveller as well as the local people about the antiquities of the town. Tourism had arrived and Shrewsbury's position on the road into Wales brought many to the town en route to the scenes of sublime grandeur beyond Llangollen which so horrified and delighted the sensitive students of the Picturesque.

Race-meetings, balls, military displays and gatherings, public executions, the Theatre, weekly markets, horse fairs, frenzied local Parliamentary elections where the burgesses' votes were bought and the ballot rigged, subscription libraries, newspaper offices and reading rooms, freak shows and itinerant showmen such as the local 'flyer' Robert Cadman, made Shrewsbury a lively town in which to live. Eighteenth-century Shrewsbury was an impressive place; it repays exploration on foot.

Thomas Telford considered that the town owed its prosperity to its position on the River Severn. The transportation of goods up from the sea port of Bristol, which had extensive coastal traffic as well as overseas trade, meant that virtually all goods could be easily and cheaply obtained in Shrewsbury. Local produce was exported by the same route; most of the cheap Welsh cloth finished in Shrewsbury at this time was shipped to the West Indies and South America to clothe slaves. The river was navigable as far as Welshpool, but it was (and is) unpredictable; it rose rapidly and flooded regularly and could also become too low for even the shallow-draught Upper Severn trows designed to operate on its hazardous waters. The numerous permanent fishweirs constructed across the main stream had to be by-passed by the trows through cuttings such as that still traceable at Coton Hill. The gangs of men, the bow-haulers, which appear in several 18th- and early 19th-century illustrations, had a brutish life pulling the loaded barges upstream from the estuary; they were notorious for their riotous behaviour in their off duty hours which were usually spent in riverside pubs. Three quays catered for the loading and unloading of goods; these were at Mardol, Frankwell and by the English Bridge, but other points around the river were also used such as Chadlode and Cordlode in the Quarry. The barges, often showing sails, appear in many early views and were obviously an important part of the townscape just as they played an essential part in the town's economy. They were also built and repaired here, providing work for ropemakers, sailmakers, carpenters and the many other crafts associated with boats. This aspect of the town's 18th-century life has left virtually no sign that it ever existed; however, the Welsh Bridge still displays some mysterious iron tackle among its elegant stone balusters; this was used to haul the trows, with their masts lowered, under the navigation arch of the bridge before they could tie up at Mardol or Frankwell quays.

Waterborne goods were the cheapest while roads were poorly maintained and carts were inadequate for large or heavy loads, so canals were constructed where rivers could not be made to serve the purpose. The Shrewsbury Canal was built at the end of the 18th century to transport goods and material, particularly coal from east Shropshire, to and from the town. A site by the canal a mile or so north of the castle was chosen for a surprisingly large factory building of revolutionary construction in 1796-7. This was a flax mill which used cast-iron columns, beams and window frames in place of wood to reduce the risk of fire in what was known to be a hazardous branch of manufacture. It is now recognised as the earliest example of an iron-framed building in the world and therefore of immense interest; it was not, however, the forerunner of large-scale industrialisation in the town.

Many towns of similar size to Shrewsbury were transformed by industrialisation in the 19th century. The reasons why this failed to happen here have not been fully investigated, but the history of Marshall's flax mill and a similar slightly later enterprise at Castle Fields provides some clues. The Ditherington factory was operated by a family who were committed socially and politically to Leeds where they had other premises; the Shrewsbury mill took second place in their enterprise. The Castle Fields mill was poorly managed by local men who were not fully committed to making it a success. Without this commitment to their factories, social eminence in the community or the ability to affect local political conditions, it was unlikely that local industrialists, however revolutionary their approach to buildings and machinery might be, could establish a basis on which large-scale industrialisation could occur. In the case of local woollen cloth production, there were strong vested interests in maintaining domestic production rather than establishing a factory system. The local population figures show that the workforce was not increasing rapidly, which would also have restricted any attempts at widescale industrial expansion. Other evidence suggests that Shrewsbury was already attracting retired people living on investments or a pension; a social group which would not extend the labour force available to entrepreneurs.

This early failure of industrialisation has affected the history of the town ever since. It did not mean that there was no employment in industries in the town; on the contrary, there were many workshops established in the 19th century, but the large-scale heavy industrial works which led to the transformation of many midland towns into grand Victorian cities passed Shrewsbury by.

By all accounts, the town in the early 19th century was a backward-looking, unmodernised, insanitary place. Progress to improve its lighting, street-surfacing and cleaning, water supply, drainage and sewerage was to prove painfully slow. The filthy open streets were used for all the local markets; fruit, green vegetables, hay, corn, fish, poultry, cheese and butter, meat, sheep, cattle, pigs and horses. Butchers slaughtered their animals in Butcher Row and Pride Hill. Most of the water available to the inhabitants was pumped from the river which also carried away any of the town's rubbish and sewage which was not left festering in the streets, alleyways and courts. It is not surprising that the town's state of health was below the national average. A detailed report made by an inspector from the General Board of Health in 1854 reveals the true horror of conditions in Shrewsbury which had probably existed for centuries; it corrects any illusions we may have derived from the Romantically idealised paintings, drawings and prints which survive in large numbers from the first half of the 19th century.

The brief period of Shrewsbury's importance as a major staging post on the reconstructed Holyhead Road did much to revive the town at a period when other sources of wealth, notably the Welsh cloth trade, were failing. Business and pleasure travellers took advantage of the increased speed and comfort of coach travel on Telford's improved highway. However, these same people took even more enthusiastically to the cheaper, faster and more comfortable train services when these became available in the 1830s and 1840s. Chester took over Shrewsbury's position on the London-Dublin route when rail services were opened. The failure of the linen mills and the loss of the Holyhead Road trade were reasons given for the fall in Shrewsbury's population in 1831 and 1841.

The railway finally arrived in Shrewsbury in 1848 in the form of a branch line from, aptly enough, the rival city of Chester. Other lines rapidly linked the town with Birmingham, Hereford, Crewe, Worcester, Aberystwyth and Stafford. The railway companies operating through Shrewsbury all needed extensive engine and goods sheds, sidings and other facilities, but joined together to operate the handsome neo-Tudor railway station. A rogue company, the Potteries, Shrewsbury and North Wales Railway was forced by the existing companies to construct its own terminus opposite the Abbey and to run on its own track; this crippling requirement led to the railway's early closure in 1880 after a few years of ruinous business. Little destruction was necessary to bring the railways close to the town centre unlike other ancient towns; the Castle Hill area, which was literally carted off, was rundown and unhealthy though no more so than many other parts of town. The loss of the open space called the Dana was particularly obvious to the crowds that had invariably gathered there to watch executions above the gatehouse of the County Gaol.

After a long period of decline in the 18th century, Shrewsbury School experienced a steady increase in pupils through the 19th century due largely to the ability of Samuel Butler, the headmaster from 1798. Expectations of living accommodation and school facilities, however, changed radically during the century which led to the Castle Gates site being regarded as hopelessly inadequate to all but diehard Old Salopians. In 1882 the School moved to the Foundling Hospital/House of Industry premises overlooking the town on Kingsland. The Borough of Shrewsbury opened its Free Library and Museum in the old school premises.

New public buildings appeared in various parts of the town. The Music Hall was built to provide accommodation for a variety of events as well as to house post and stamp offices, the police station and a newspaper reading room. Small market halls were built in Howard Street, Bridge Street and Pride Hill to provide shelter for people selling dairy produce, but they were superseded in 1869 by the imposing General Market which brought all the street markets under one roof for the first time. In 1850, the marshy ground below Castle Street and Pride Hill was raised to provide a large Smithfield for livestock sales, thereby freeing the streets of the hazards of large numbers of sheep, pigs, cattle and horses on market days; the animals were, however, still herded through the town centre to the Smithfield until well into this century when motor vehicles took over this job. An Armoury was built to house safely the guns and ammunition of the Militia at the time of the Napoleonic Wars; this was followed in 1870 by a large Barracks in Copthorne which was finally vacated by the Light Infantry in 1984. The Salop Infirmary, having outgrown its 18th-century home, was rebuilt in 1830 incorporating the latest improvements in ventilation. An uncompromisingly Victorian Eye Hospital, overlooking the Quarry, was opened in 1881. After years of campaigning by townspeople concerned at the high death rate through drowning in the treacherous Severn, swimming baths were opened in 1894.

As with most towns, the 19th century saw a steady expansion of housing into the suburbs, but in Shrewsbury this was piecemeal and haphazard so these suburbs are pleasantly varied and socially mixed. Kingsland is an exception in that it was a development promoted by the Borough of Shrewsbury to appeal to the wealthiest section of town society; the huge dark red-brick school houses and private villas set among mature trees make this area unlike any other part of the town. Anglican churches were built cheaply in an attempt to offset the attractions of the chapels and gospel missions which flourished in the new suburbs. One of these churches, Holy Trinity in Coleham, exemplifies an important change in the way people lived. It was built in 1836 as a base for missionary work among the hard-drinking workers from the leadworks, foundry and brewery of this ancient riverside suburb; within a few decades, the church was totally rebuilt to suit the more genteel taste of parishioners in the new Victorian suburb of Belle Vue, many of whom had left the cramped living quarters over town centre shops for the semi-rural calm of the suburb.

This process of migration from overcrowded, insanitary town centre properties was greatly expedited by the Borough in the 20th century, notably by clearing the slums in and around Barker Street. Council estates were built to house those displaced by this major scheme which was prompted by the increase in motor traffic and the need for car parking.

The Sentinel Waggon Works and the Chatwood Safe Company built new estates for their employees to the north of the town. The Borough Council was also responsible, to its lasting credit, for the magnificent reconstruction of the English Bridge. Wyle Cop was widened at the bridge end and opposite the *Lion* to cope with increased traffic. In 1924, the Castle was purchased and given to the town by the Shropshire Horticultural Society, which has enriched the town in numerous ways from the proceeds of the hugely successful annual Flower Show which brings thousands to the Quarry from a wide area.

The Second World War caused negligible damage to the town, but the combined effects of Merseyside evacuees, Italian prisoners of war, U.S. Air Force personnel and service men and women from all parts of Britain broadened the perspectives of many townspeople. Cinemas, dance halls and pubs could barely cope with the demands of soldiers and airmen based near the town. House prices were high and local shops did excellent business in unrationed goods. The *Raven Hotel* became the American Red Cross Club on 4 July 1943; its luxurious bars, games rooms and appetising food were regarded enviously by British servicemen from their own club opposite which was 'a dingy old shop selling rock cakes and tea'. On the edge of the town, the bypass was closed in 1943 for the duration of the war to be used as a storage depot for up to 1,500 military vehicles.

The planners of Shrewsbury since the war must bear the responsibility for some notable mistakes, but these would have been more numerous had the commercial pressure for change been greater. Other towns have suffered more severely. The majority of schemes to change the ancient townscape have merely been discussed for decades and then abandoned. The result is a modern town functioning in an unusually rich collection of buildings and spaces which have been bequeathed to us by our predecessors.

The illustrations in this book have been arranged to correspond with the town's topography. Views of the river Severn introduce four groups of illustrations which each have their starting point at the junction of Castle Street and Pride Hill, the site of the High Cross.

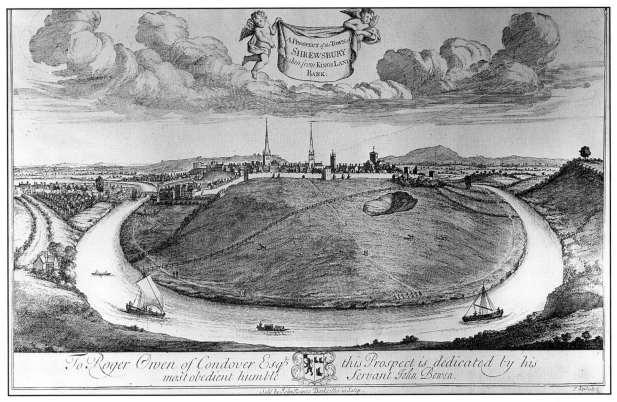

1 This early 18th-century panorama shows the town from Kingsland. In the Quarry can be seen the great hollow from which stone was extracted in the medieval period. Seven bow-haulers are dragging a trow upriver while another, under sail, is heading in the opposite direction. A ferry is in operation by the *Boat House*.

2 A detail of the previous print shows boats moored by Frankwell Quay and boat-building by the Austin Friars.

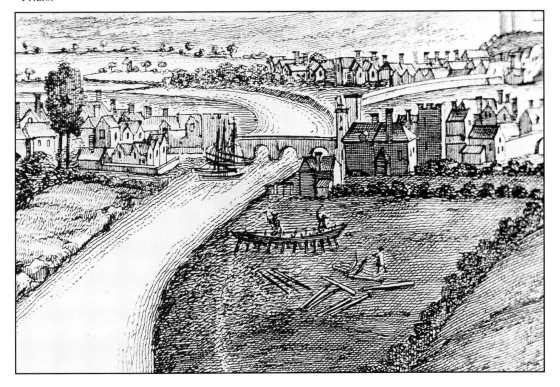

3 Trows seen from Coton Hill *c*.1840. A Romanticised picture of an improbably wide river Severn, but an interesting record of the latter days of the Severn Navigation. Since 1809 the boats had been pulled upriver by horses.

4 This early 18th-century print shows two trows tied up at Stone Bridge Quay. This wharf was known earlier as Bulgerlode; it has been suggested that this name was derived from boulgers, makers of leather bags and pouches, who may have worked nearby at the foot of Wyle Cop.

5 The *Boat House*, Frankwell, in 1891. This timber-framed building was used to isolate plague victims from St Chad's parish in 1650 and was presumably old at that date. It later became a public house and was popular with bargees and watermen operating the trows.

6 The Foundling Hospital building of 1760-5, designed by Thomas Farnolls Pritchard, was a branch of the London institution. At one time it housed 400 orphans but closed in 1774. It was taken over as the town's workhouse when the five parishes incorporated in an effort to reduce poor rates in 1784.

7 *Prince of Wales* pub opposite the Quarry *c.*1875. One of the town boat clubs, the Pengwern founded in 1871, had its headquarters at Evans' Boat House next to the pub.

8 Fish weirs on the Severn were valued properties for centuries, but they caused navigational difficulties. This weir at Preston Boats survived until 1910 probably because the eels it trapped were much in demand by Shrewsbury townspeople.

9 River Severn, August 1881. Before the weir was built in 1910-2, the river level could fall very low in summer. As the town's sewage was discharged directly into the river, the consequences of little or no water flow can be imagined. In earlier times, the low water level halted river traffic.

10 Pride Hill *c*.1850. The neo-classical building on the left was the Butter Market as rebuilt in 1844. A General Post Office replaced it in 1875.

11 Pride Hill has always been one of the town's main shopping streets. It was also, until 1982, part of the main traffic route through the town. The decorations in the photograph were to celebrate the coronation of George VI in 1937.

12   The hill is thought to be named after the influential Pride family whose medieval stone mansion probably stood close to the shops on the right in this 1911 view.

13 The street at the lower end of Pride Hill was also called Single Butcher Row on the left side and Shoemakers or Corvisors Row on the right. The unbearable stench coming from the butchers' premises here and in (Double) Butcher Row as they boiled down offal sometimes forced Pride Hill shopkeepers to close early.

14 Ireland's Mansion, High Street. This is the most impressive of the Elizabethan timber-framed buildings which still stand in the town centre. Most of them were built by influential Shrewsbury drapers who controlled the Welsh wool trade.

15 High Street, *c*.1865. Owen's Mansion of 1592 faces Ireland's Mansion. At the bottom of Pride Hill can be seen Edward Edward's shop; he was also licensee of the *Bull* in Abbey Foregate. He worked for Disraeli during his 1841 election campaign to become one of Shrewsbury's M.Ps.

16 In 1961 the extensive remains of one of the town's medieval stone mansions, Bennett's Hall, was revealed at the foot of Pride Hill. It was incorporated in a new shop on the site.

17 High Street *c*.1900. Della Porta's (later Rackham's) department store was built on the site of the shops on the right of the photograph in 1929. The Presbyterian chapel had had to be rebuilt at Government expense after its demolition by an anti-Government mob in 1715.

18 Lloyd's Mansion 1903. Della Porta's shop was opened in 1857 in Princess Street and later extended into these premises. The firm described itself as 'complete home furnisher and universal provider'.

19   The Square, seen here in 1923, became the town's market place for grain, fruit and vegetables *c*.1260. Shortly afterwards, the Booth or Guild Hall was built across the Square where Lord Clive's statue now stands. The old market hall was built in 1596 to give cover to corn dealers and to provide a room above for Welsh cloth sales.

20 The horse-drawn, steam-powered fire engine of the amalgamated insurance companies outside its base at Franklin's Livery stable in Cross Hill.

21 Square 1836. The Salop Fire Office, which insured many Shropshire properties as is evident from the metal fire marks or plaques still attached to them, had its office and kept its fire engines, ladders and hooks handy on the site later occupied by the Music Hall.

22 Salop Old Bank in the Square 1888. The building opened in 1792 as the Shrewsbury Bank. It was managed by Rocke, Eyton and Co. Lloyds Bank acquired the local firm and the bank was closed in 1922.

23 The north side of the Square was formerly the place where the drapers' shops were located and was known as the Drapery or the Shields. The *Plough Inn*, later enlarged, occupied part of the site in 1888.

24 St Mary's church, *c*.1890. The church was a royal foundation long before the Norman Conquest. The building has examples of all medieval styles of architecture, notably the nave arcades of *c*.1200. It also has a superb 14th-century English Jesse window which was moved here from Old St Chad's church when it collapsed in 1788.

25 In a gale in early 1894 the top section of St Mary's spire crashed through the nave roof causing much damage. The spires of St Alkmund's and St Mary's had for centuries attracted daredevil antics. On one occasion, a travelling showman, Robert Cadman, died when he came off a rope he was 'flying' down from the top of St Mary's spire to the Gay Meadow on the opposite bank of the Severn.

26 Facing St Mary's church is the Hall built in 1576-82 by the Drapers' Guild whose members controlled virtually all aspects of the town's government and economy in the reign of Elizabeth I.

27 The Salop Infirmary was founded in 1745 in an empty private house in St Mary's Place. It was rebuilt in 1830. This view of *c.*1907 overlooks the Gay Meadow.

28 In the mid 19th-century Butcher Row was still occupied by butchers. The slaughtering of animals in the street and in the yards off it caused great offence to people working and living nearby. The nuisance continued until a municipal abattoir was opened near the Smithfield. This early morning view of *c*.1893 features an impressive four-storied gabled building since demolished.

29 This building stood between Butcher Row and St Alkmund's church. Access to the graveyard was through a passage called Burying Shut which can be seen above the pram. The brazen shop advertising belongs to a less squeamish age than our own.

30 Butcher Row 1891. The exceptionally fine 15th-century timber-framed building was built with open-fronted shops on the ground floor. It was neglected in the 19th century when it became an overcrowded tenement notorious for the depravity of its occupants.

31 Old St Alkmund's church was the result of several centuries of piecemeal rebuilding and additions.

32 St Alkmund's church 1891. The church was rebuilt 1794-5. It was transformed into an elegant Gothick preaching chamber, a suitable theatre in which its famous and popular Irish vicar, Richard de Courcy, could perform his much-admired extempore sermons. The plaster ceiling by Joseph Bromfield and most of the cast-iron windows made by the Coalbrookdale Company were later removed.

33 The Rev. Charles Wightman was vicar of St Alkmund's from 1841 to 1893. His wife Julia is remembered for her efforts to provide alternatives to public houses for the poor of the parish, many of whose lives were ruined by drink.

34 Fish Street, *c*.1910. The ladies are painting the view looking down Grope Lane, a favourite subject with artists. Above them, in the centre, can be seen the rear elevation of the huge 15th-century timber-framed building featured in illustration 30.

35 Fish Street, *c*.1912. W.B. Walker's County printing offices produced ledgers and other business stationery in these premises beside Grope Lane. The craftsman and his apprentice are operating a machine which printed ruled sheets for account books. Printing had been an important trade in Shrewsbury in the 18th century when many books in Welsh were published here.

36 Fish Street in 1891. Until the mid-13th century Shrewsbury's markets were held in the cemetery of St Alkmund's and St Julian's churches seen here in the distance.

37 Fish Street, *c*.1910. The fish merchants had stalls in this street from the 14th to the 19th centuries. Butchers from the country around Shrewsbury were also allowed to sell here until the opening of the General Market in 1869 which brought street markets to an end.

38 St Julian's church in 1891. In 1749-50 the church was rebuilt to the design of Thomas Farnolls Pritchard who also designed the Iron Bridge at Coalbrookdale. The ceiling was decorated with some of the wooden bosses from the old church.

39 In 1846 the south elevation of St Julian's church was 'embellished', as the Georgian church was considered too plain. The view from the street had been opened up in 1789 when some houses between the church and the street were pulled down.

40 Milk Street in 1911. Milk Street once extended from High Street as far as Town Walls, but the inhabitants of the elegant newly-built southern part of the street adopted the name Belmont for their section in the late 18th century.

41 At the High Street end of Milk Street stood the Shearmen's Guild Hall. The shearmen processed the Welsh cloth purchased by the drapers; they were numerous but poorly paid. Their determination to celebrate May Day outside their hall in 1589 caused much trouble with the town's Puritan faction.

42 The ancient parish church of St Chad collapsed early in the morning of 9 July 1788. The tower had been undermined by recent burials in the church.

43 Belmont, *c*.1937. The escort of the Corporate Officers of the Borough, the Bellman, Mace-bearers, Sergeants at mace and Sword-bearer waiting for the Assize Judge to come from his Lodging before processing to the courts in the Shirehall in the Square.

44 Only one of the many medieval interval towers on the town walls survives. It has been lived in for centuries, notably by a local clockmaker, John Massey, and his family in 1816.

45 Swan Hill 1942. A rare wartime photograph. Uniformed military personnel outside the *Admiral Benbow* which was originally the *Talbot Inn* tap for the servants of the gentry staying at the inn across the street. The kerbs have been painted to help drivers navigate the winding streets in the blackout.

46 Princess Street, *c.*1921. Originally named after the chandlers or candle makers who worked here, the narrow street leads to Old St Chad's church and the remains of its college of priests who celebrated masses for the wealthy townspeople who had endowed chantries for this purpose. On the left can be seen the ancient *Bell Inn* which was used by carriers from Ludlow and Bishop's Castle.

47 Princess Street, *c*.1916. Lloyd's Mansion of 1570 had many of the characteristic features of local timber-framed buildings of Elizabeth I's reign; a school of carpenters created a distinctive local style. The roof was of slate from Harnage near Shrewsbury.

48 St John's Hill, *c*.1896. The grandiose Market building was best seen from this vantage point. This unfashionable end of the street contained a mixture of tradesmen, plumbers and chimney sweeps as well as a printing works and the *Shrewsbury Chronicle* newspaper offices. An earlier name, Pig Hill, records the site of the Swine Market in the 17th and 18th centuries.

49 St Chad's church was rebuilt on a new site between 1790 and 1792. It sits awkwardly among some of the town's finest Georgian houses, but is itself a distinguished church building. It was designed by George Steuart who was already known locally through his work at Attingham Park and Lythwood Hall.

50 The interior of St Chad's was criticised from the outset as being too like a theatre, but as the parish was the largest in the town and the church was designed to seat 1,600 this may have been inevitable. The sermon was the most important element in Anglican observance at the time and the church was clearly designed so that its congregation could see and hear the preacher.

51 Hercules, *c*.1870. This Italian lead statue has occupied at least four locations in the town; its position at the entrance to the Quarry probably showed it to best advantage, but some mid-Victorian Salopians thought it indecent to have him so near a place of public worship. The man in uniform was a Shrewsbury Borough policeman.

52 Public baths opened in the Quarry in 1894. First and second class baths were alternately available for men and women. Mixed bathing was first allowed, as an experiment, in 1927.

53 and **54** Shrewsbury Flower Show draws huge crowds every year to the town. Queen Mary visited it in 1927 and inspected the county war memorial unveiled in 1922.

55 Mardol Head, *c*.1865. An exceptional group of buildings stood between Shoplatch and Claremont Street at the junction of Mardol and Mardol Head until demolished in 1867. The narrow entry to Shoplatch, also called Carriers End, was causing traffic problems by this time.

56 Mardol Head in 1923. A comparison with photograph 55 shows how Shoplatch was widened when the General Market was built in 1867-9. The Holyhead-London signposts are a reminder that the main road still passed through the town centre.

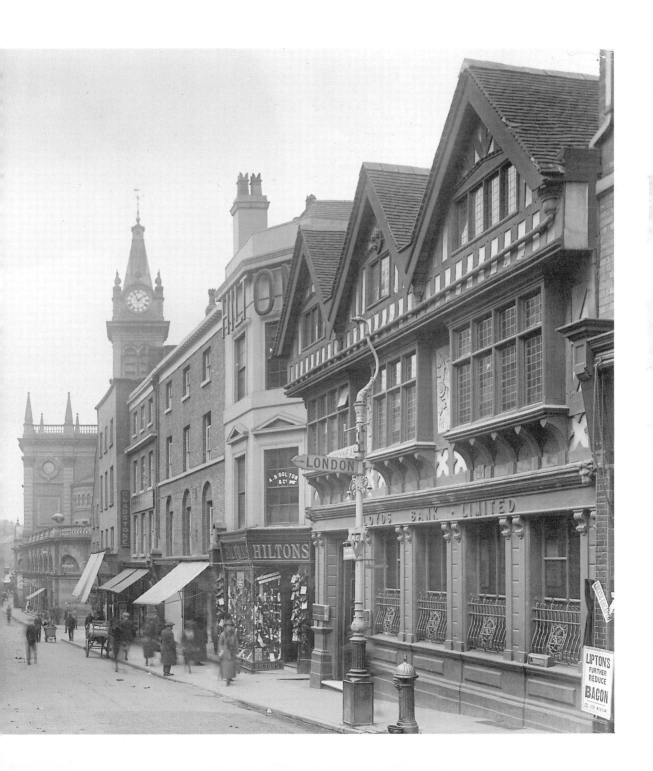

57 The Market possessed a tower 151 ft. high containing a bell. Sir Nikolaus Pevsner wrote of the building 'the chief Victorian contribution to public architecture in the town, and not one to be proud of'.

58 A theatre had existed on the same site in Shoplatch since 1765. It was rebuilt in 1834 and underwent several changes including conversion to a cinema until it burned out in June 1945.

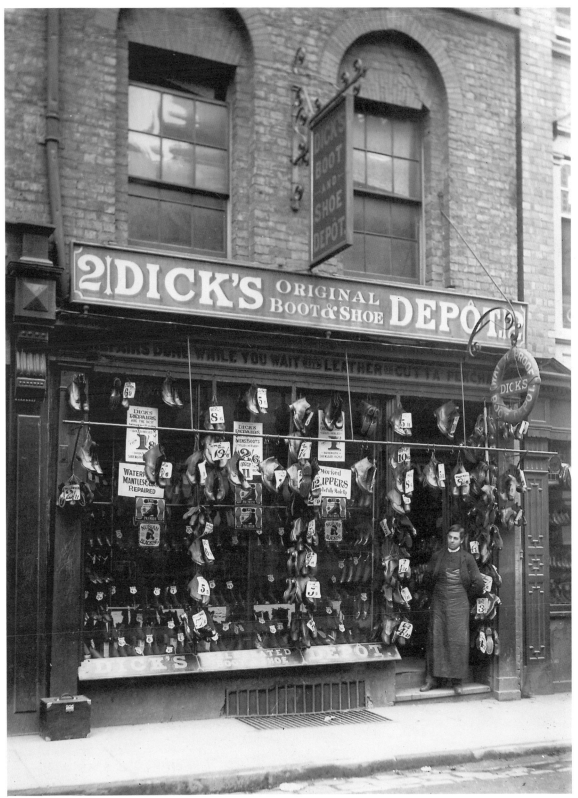

59 Victorian shop displays put as many goods as possible on the pavement to attract passers-by. A remarkable series of over 100 shops and their staff was recorded by Joseph Lewis Della Porta in 1888. This view of a shoe shop in Shoplatch includes his box of photographic plates.

60 and **61**   The Market site, *c.*1867. Local photographers recorded all stages of this redevelopment project which was on an unprecedented scale.

62 Shoplatch, c.1898. On market days this street was busy with country people and locals using nearby dining-rooms, oyster bars, pubs and stabling.

63 Inside the Market Hall local produce was on offer in what was known as the 'pannier' market after the baskets in which goods were carried, often for many miles, usually by women.

64 The Market Hall was also used as a market for locally produced cheese, as here in the 1930s.

65 Dissenting meeting houses of many different sorts were established in the town. This neat Baptist chapel was built in Claremont Street in 1780 in the garden of Cole Hall, one of Shrewsbury medieval stone houses, but needed enlarging 30 years later.

66 This photograph taken in the Corn Exchange records the granting of the Freedom of the Borough to William Phillips in 1903. Phillips was a local historian who gave much of his time to preserving the town's archives. The photograph shows the Mayor and Corporation proudly embodying the centuries-old authority vested in them.

67 John Frail (1804-1879) was a barber who had his shop at the corner of Claremont Street and Mardol. He had a hand in most aspects of town life notably the management of the Racecourse; he was thought to fix races, elections, court cases and anything else he could influence.

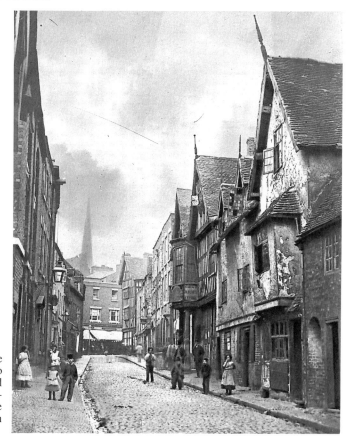

68 Claremont Street 1865. All the buildings on the right side of the street were about to be demolished to make way for the new Market. They included several remarkable timber-framed buildings and some fine 18th-century brick houses. The Shrewsbury branch of the London Foundling Hospital was first set up here in 1759.

69 Bellstone in 1867. The anonymous photographer recording the demolition has the full attention of the onlookers. The Theatre building of 1834 is visible in the distance. A large glacial boulder, now in a yard off Bellstone, has been in this vicinity for centuries but may not be the origin of the street name.

70 Barker Street, 1934. This photograph records a totally vanished scene. The Claremont Street Baptist chapel railings on the right provide the only remaining fixed point. All these properties were about to be demolished to widen the approach to the Welsh Bridge and to provide a car park.

71 Barker Street, *c*.1930. Three carved stones have been built into cottages on the site of Rombaldsham Hall which was demolished *c*.1760. The stones formed parts of a chimneypiece in the old house which had belonged to a wealthy Tudor family named Montgomery. The exact nature of Rombaldsham, an area of the town which is mentioned in medieval records, remains unclear.

72 When the Welsh Bridge was rebuilt downstream from its original position in 1796, the street leading to it, formerly Cripplelode, was renamed Bridge Street. The *Old Ship Inn*, in the middle of this photograph, belonged to the Harwood family who also owned the *Boat House Inn*. As they also owned trows and barges, it is likely that the inn was used by the men who worked the boats from Bristol to Welshpool.

73 The central building in this Mardol Head group was five storeys high. Though timber-framed, it had been covered with decorative plasterwork known as pargetting, a rare occurrence in this part of the country.

74 Mardol in 1888 had many small businesses such as this ironmonger's. Its Gothick shopfront was particularly elegant.

75 Mardol in 1891. The street was for centuries an important shopping thoroughfare linking the western gate, on the Welsh Bridge, to the centre of the town. The meaning of its name has not been unravelled.

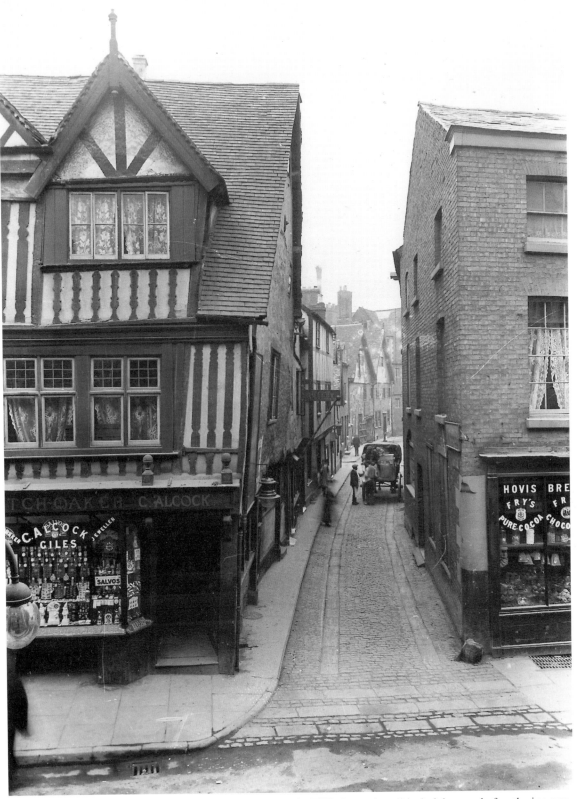

76 The horse and cart is stopped outside the *Gullet Inn* in Hill's Lane. A political club named after the inn was founded here in 1785. Local M.Ps and prominent townsmen met every Tuesday evening.

77 The four-storey building in the centre of the photograph was the home of William Rowley, a wealthy draper who speculated in the development of Barbados in the Caribbean. He built it in 1618. It is thought to have been Shrewsbury's first house built of brick. It was later lived in by John Hill, Mayor in 1688; the street, Hill's Lane, is named after him.

78 Rowley's Mansion had become surrounded by squalid property by 1808 when it was being used as a woollen manufactory, and it was to decline further until it was saved from demolition during slum clearance of the area in the 1930s.

79 William Rowley occupied the timber-framed house next to his mansion when he first came to Shrewsbury. This huge building had become almost lost in a warren of courts and passages, but it was rescued in the 1930s when the area was cleared; its poor condition is all too evident in this view of *c*.1930.

80   Singleton and Coles made cigarettes and cigars in extensive works between Mardol and Hill's Lane between 1891 and 1939. The factory had steam-driven machinery and employed a hundred staff. The wooden Indian had belonged to the earlier firm of Harries which dated back to 1802. Singleton and Coles cigarette cards are still collected by enthusiasts.

81 Mardol *c*.1870. The alleys (locally called 'shuts') between Mardol and Roushill were occupied by the town's prostitutes in the mid-19th century. The entry to one of these, Mason's Passage, is seen on the right.

82 Roushill floods possibly in 1869. Roushill was a notorious area of the town unfrequented by respectable people. The gabled building on the right was the *Horseshoe Inn* which appeared regularly in newspaper reports of prostitution cases. The photographer has been attracted by the flood to an otherwise unrecorded view.

83 From 1850 to 1959, Raven Meadows housed the town's Smithfield Market. This photograph is of the last pig sales before the market transferred to Harlescott.

84 and **85** Shrewsbury Cycle Carnival *c.*1902 in aid of the local hospitals. The participants are seen congregating in Raven Meadows. The tall chimney in one of the photographs was part of the Electricity Works which opened in 1895, but it would be several decades before most people had electricity in their homes.

Welsh Bridge Shrewsbury

86 The Welsh, or St George's, Bridge is recorded from the 13th century onwards. It had strong towers at the Frankwell end and over the arch nearest to Mardol.

87 The tower on the Welsh Bridge was a particularly impressive piece of military architecture. It featured a statue of Edward the Black Prince (d. 1376) which was transferred to the old market hall in the Square when the tower was demolished.

88 The old Welsh Bridge was only 10½ ft. wide, was difficult for river traffic to negotiate and was in poor repair. In 1792, it was decided to build a replacement which would be 28½ ft. wide.

89 The speed and sound of the mighty Severn in flood, as here in 1869, always attract much interest, but the inhabitants of Frankwell and other low-lying parts of town have had to live with the consequences of periodic flooding of their homes for centuries.

90 The site of the new bridge below the old one soon led to trouble as the river bed around its foundations was being washed away. In 1833 the bed below the bridge had to be reinforced with rubble stone, a measure which has preserved it to the present.

91 Frankwell possessed an impressive mixture of buildings which once faced the medieval Welsh Bridge and the busy quay for barges. These 18th-century buildings had declined in status by the 1930s when they were used as a cheap lodging house. Having become dangerous, they were demolished in 1946.

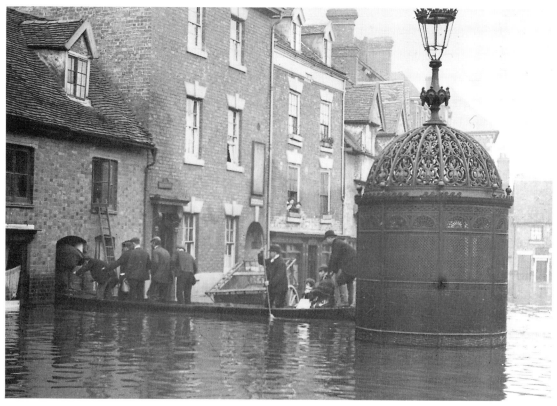

92 Flooding at Frankwell Quay, *c.*1899. Supplies are being delivered to a marooned resident, but the magnificent gentlemen's lavatory steals the show.

93 Frankwell Quay, December 1950. This unlucky motorist is attempting to back his way to safety.

94 Frankwell, the western suburb, has many fine 16th-century buildings in its streets. The name has not been explained. Though originally grand, most of the houses had become overcrowded tenements by the 19th century and the alleys behind them were dirty and unhealthy as they lacked sanitation.

95 Frankwell in 1911. The inhabitants of the 'Little Borough' were fiercely loyal to their side of the river and were dismissive of the town centre's obvious superiority.

96 This 1938 view looks down Frankwell towards the Welsh Bridge. On the right stands a large property built in 1576-7 by John Worrall. It was removed in the 1960s to make way for a traffic roundabout, but part of it was rebuilt at Avoncroft Museum.

97   The riverside meadows beyond the Mount were favourite picnic places for many boating parties. This group from the Pengwern Boat Club was photographed *c*.1910.

98 In the 18th century Castle Street was known as Raven Street after the hotel which was the chief coaching inn until 1780, when Robert Lawrence moved from there to the *Lion* on Wyle Cop taking the coach services with him. The *Ràven* is first recorded in 1520. For most of the 18th century it was the leading hostelry in Shrewsbury and was the scene of major social events.

99 The Council House is so called because the President of the Council in the Marches of Wales lived there when visiting Shrewsbury from his base at Ludlow Castle. Charles I resided there in 1642 when Shrewsbury was temporarily his headquarters. The gate near the river is the one by which Parliamentary forces were admitted after their attack on the defences below the castle. On the left of the photograph can be seen the new stone Union Wharf of 1825; river traffic was still important at this date.

100 Together with brawn, Shrewsbury 'cakes' were the most widely-known local product. Several shops sold them, but Plimmers in Castle Street retained sole rights to Pailin's secret recipe. The shop was temptingly near to the boys of Shrewsbury School until they left for Kingsland in 1882.

101 Though all but one of these buildings in Castle Street still exist, this scene is not easy to recognise. The curious brick façade on the left fronted Thornes Hall (demolished 1921), a 17th-century mansion said to have associations with Mrs. Fitzherbert, the morganatic wife of George IV.

102 In 1914 George V visited the town to attend the Royal Agricultural Show held on the Racecourse at Monkmoor. A suffragette demonstration was feared and security was particularly strong, as can be seen in this photograph of Castle Gates.

103 Shrewsbury School in 1871. The phenomenal early success of the town's Free Grammar School in attracting students led rapidly to a series of building projects between 1589 and 1630 which resulted in one of the grandest school buildings in the country. However, the site was cramped and the buildings were no longer adequate, so a move to another site was already under consideration when this photograph was taken.

104 In 1897 a statue to Shrewsbury's most famous native, Charles Darwin, was erected in front of the school he had reluctantly attended. Local feeling was divided over the wisdom of commemorating a man whose views had challenged religious orthodoxies.

105 The date and circumstances of this impromptu maypole dance are unknown, but it took place in front of the old Shrewsbury School building which was converted to a free library and museum run by the Borough of Shrewsbury in 1885.

106 John Rocque's map of 1746 demonstrates the commanding position of the Castle which occupies half the width of the narrow neck of land at the northern approach. Two earthworks are shown on Castle Hill; they may have dated from King Stephen's siege of Shrewsbury Castle in 1138.

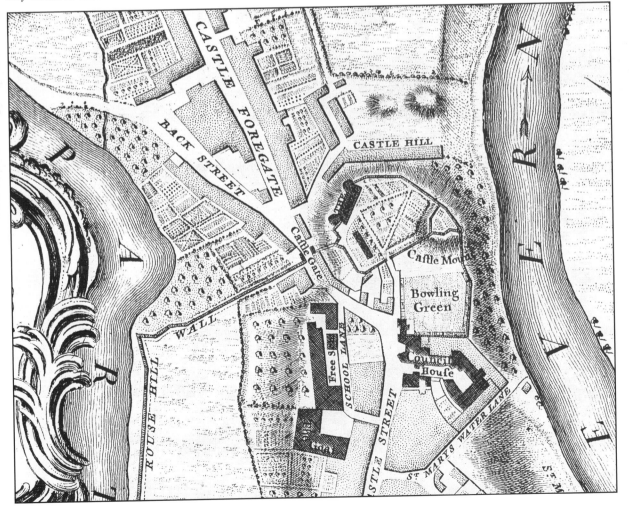

107 Castle Gates is so called because two heavily fortified stone gates defended this, the only land approach to the town. The upper gate straddled the street next to the huge stone school building seen here. It had been used as a prison but was demolished in 1825 when the street was lowered to reduce the gradient of the hill.

108 Shrewsbury Castle in 1822. The view from Castle Gates outside the outer north gate, part of which can be seen in the print. Dating from the years immediately after the Norman Conquest, the castle had an eventful history which began a new phase when it was converted into a comfortable residence for one of the town's M.Ps by the civil engineer Thomas Telford.

109 The railway station occupies the site of Castle Hill, an insalubrious warren of small cottages, and an open space, the Dana, which used to be thronged whenever a public hanging took place at the County Gaol. This print dates from the years immediately after the coming of the railway in 1848.

110 The station's close proximity to the castle is revealed in this photograph of 1948.

111 The stone bridge constructed to carry the Shrewsbury and Birmingham Railway in 1849 is recorded in this 1892 photograph. When the station was enlarged eight years later, it was concealed by new iron bridges built either side of it.

112 The station extended westwards over Castle Foregate on an iron bridge seen here *c*.1894.

113 Aenon Cottage, later rebuilt as the stationmaster's house, was given its Biblical name through its association with John Palmer, a Baptist minister, who baptised converts in the Severn below his idiosyncratic house.

114 An unusual advertising postcard showing the workroom of John Kerry's tailors in Chester Street in 1911. Mr Kerry claimed that his 'workroom is acknowledged to be the best in the Midland counties'.

115 Coton Hill, *c*.1905. St Mary's Vicarage was also known as Benbow House after the national hero Admiral John Benbow, who was born in a house on the site *c*.1653.

116 and **117**   The Ditherington flax mill constructed with an iron frame in 1796-7 after it had been converted to a maltings by William Jones and Son. Most of its original windows were bricked up to provide the correct level of light for the malting process. The Shrewsbury Canal ran alongside the factory.

118 The maltings, with its own railway access, was the largest industrial group of buildings in the town in its day, but it employed far fewer than the flax mill had at its peak in the 1840s when it provided work for 800 people.

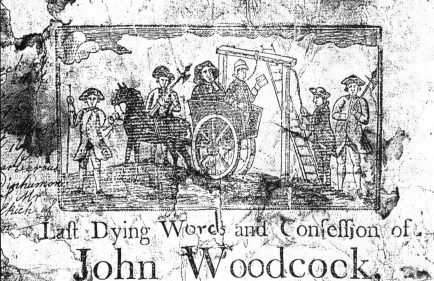

Last Dying Words and Confession of

John Woodcock,

s executed at the Old-Heath, near Shrewsbury, on Thursday the of August 1793, for the barbarous, bloody, and inhuman MURDER Mr. JOHN WOOLRICH, of Audlem, in Cheshire, on his Return me from Drayton Fair.

THE unfortunate sufferer, JOHN WOODCOCK, now only twenty-six years of age, was born at Broomhall Green, about four miles from Nantwich, in the County of Chester; and by trade a Brick-maker.

The fact for which he suffers, was committed in October 1792, as will appear by the following Narrative.

JOHN WOODCOCK, being suspected as a party concerned in the Murder of Mr. Woolrich, the most diligent enquiry was made to discover

and brought the hankerchief, triumphing in his villainy;—they then made the best of their way to Woore, where they stopped all night;—some words arose relative to dividing the plunder, but his companions having in question took care his divident should be but trifling, and they absconded him the next day. Strong reflection so troubled his mind that he could not rest, and he then went to Manchester in search of employ."

He was committed to Salop Gaol,

119 Until the construction of the County Gaol in 1793, public hangings took place at Old Heath, just north of the town. These events were always popular and souvenir 'last words' (usually fictitious) sold quickly.

120 The siting of an R.A.F. Mechanical Transport Depot at Harlescott in the First World War led indirectly to the suburban development of the area between the wars.

121 Sundorne Castle was one of several local country houses which were rebuilt during the early 19th-century enthusiasm for medieval chivalry and architecture. The estate had formerly belonged to nearby Haughmond Abbey, the remains of which had themselves been turned into a private house after the abbey had been dissolved.

122 Battlefield church 1790. The church was built to commemorate those who died at the Battle of Shrewsbury in 1403. It served a small number of parishioners and had almost become a ruin by this time.

123 The church was extensively restored in 1861-2, but is now redundant. Its remoteness and its history make it an evocative reminder of a tragic and decisive battle in English history.

124 Dogpole, *c.*1870. The Shropshire Eye and Ear Dispensary moved to Dogpole in 1866 to occupy a former home for the reformation of prostitutes. In 1881 it moved again to the newly-built hospital in Murivance.

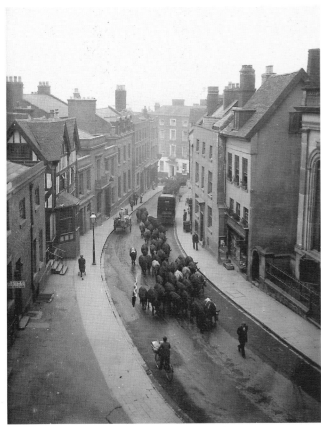

125 Dogpole, *c.*1930. Tuesdays and Fridays were market days for cattle, pigs and sheep. They were often led on foot through the town centre streets to the Smithfield in Raven Meadows.

126 Dogpole, 1888. Most items were still produced locally by craftsmen in the 19th century. George Mountford's coach and carriage works, founded in 1819, was one of three in the town.

127 The Assembly Room at the *Lion Hotel* was completed *c*.1777. It is one of the finest surviving examples and was the scene of innumerable balls, concerts and other notable public occasions.

128 Wyle Cop, a steep, narrow, curving hill, presented coach traffic on the Holyhead Road with a challenge. Thomas Telford proposed removing the north side of the road altogether and building an arched viaduct from the English Bridge to the top of the Cop.

129 In 1963 electrical heating cables were laid in the road surface of Wyle Cop which could be switched on in icy weather, surely one of the craziest schemes proposed for the town. Other utilities soon shredded the cables in their periodic roadworks.

130 These ragged boys, representative of a large section of Shrewsbury's working population, were photographed outside Blunt's the chemist on Wyle Cop in May 1889. They seem to be waiting for a procession.

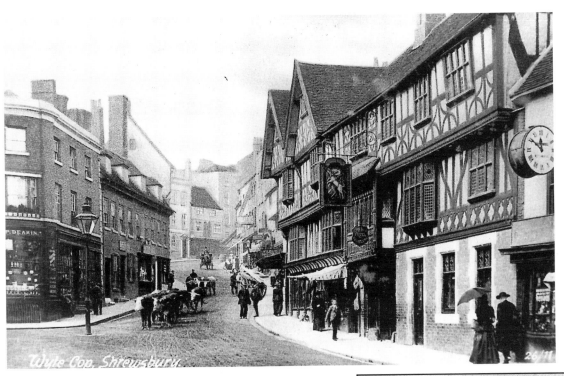

131 Wyle Cop is lined by a variety of old buildings which make this a most impressive eastern approach to the town. The bucolic peace of this scene, however, has long since succumbed to incessant traffic.

132 At the junction of St Julian's Friars and Beeches Lane at the bottom of Wyle Cop was a factory which had housed Burr's lead works until 1841; this had then moved to Kingsland where it caused ill health among its Coleham workers and death to animals grazing near it.

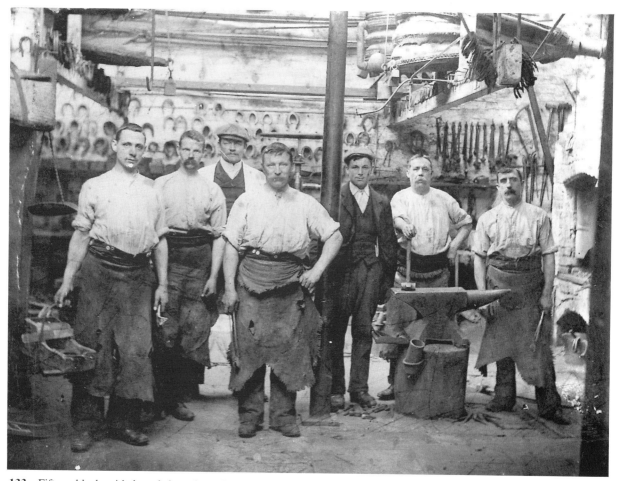

133 Fifteen blacksmiths' workshops kept the town's horses properly shod at the turn of the century. These men worked at E. Davies' smithy 'the oldest established Shrewsbury shoeing forge' on Beeches Lane.

134 St Julian's Friars, *c.*1910. Of the town's three friaries only a small section of the Franciscan friary still stands, picturesquely converted into cottages. Of its church, which once contained the huge Jesse window now in St Mary's, no details are yet known.

135 English Bridge, *c*.1880. The steepness of the old bridge caused difficulties as early as 1775 when the roadway at the centre of the bridge was lowered, but it remained a problem.

136 English Bridge, *c*.1920. The bridge was only 23½ ft. wide between the balustrades.

137 The Stone Bridge, 1770. This print records the construction of the arches of the new bridge to the left while the remaining medieval arches with three-storey houses on them still stand. Also clearly visible is the waterwheel of the engine which forced river water for domestic use to the cistern at the top of Pride Hill.

138 English Bridge, 1927. The rebuilt bridge is nearing completion. Though cranes manoeuvred the blocks of stone, most of the work was done by manual labour. Horses and carts and wheelbarrows moved tons of material.

139 English Bridge, February 1926. The bridge almost demolished. Key stones from its arches have been stacked on the small island on the left.

140 English Bridge, 1825. This view also shows the bridge over the Rea Brook built in 1795 for £450 by John Carline and John Tilley.

141 (*top left*) Coleham Head, 1927. The widened English Bridge was nearly complete when this photograph was taken. The *Swan Inn* (recorded from 1650) was delicensed in 1928 and demolished soon after. The architect John Carline's house, which faces the camera, was part of Shrewsbury Technical School at this date.

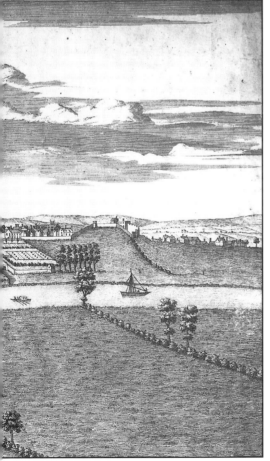

142 (*left*) In this print of *c*.1718 the Abbey Bridge extending to Coleham Head can be seen in the foreground, lined with houses. It disappeared entirely in 1772 when this branch of the Rea Brook was stopped and the road level was raised.

143 (*above*) When the English Bridge was widened and rebuilt between 1925 and 1927, the contractors used a yard by the Abbey to store the marked and numbered stones from the dismantled bridge. A lodge in the centre of the photograph protected the masons as they prepared the old and new stones for positioning. The railway was for a crane which moved the stones around the site.

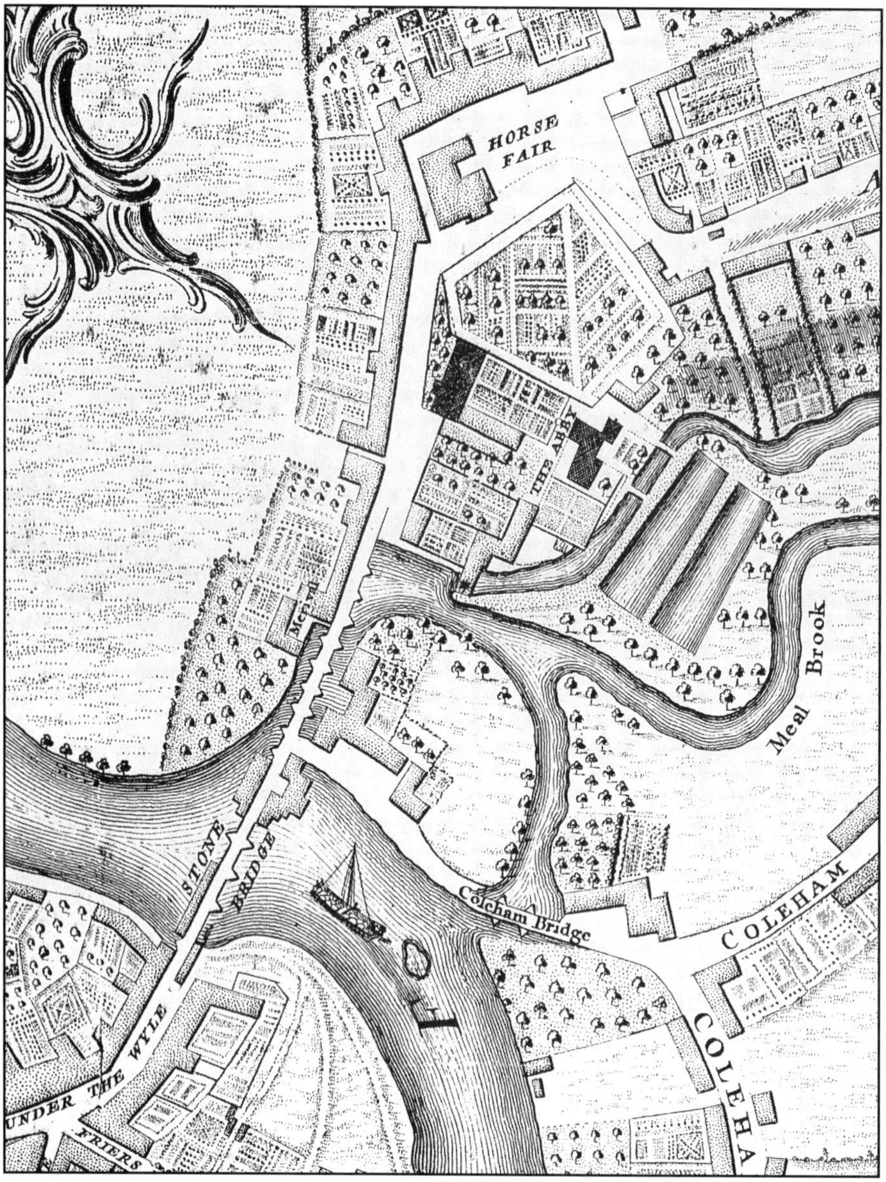
HORSE FAIR
THE ABBY
Meal Brook
STONE BRIDGE
Colcham Bridge
COLEHAM
COLEHA
UNDER THE WYLE
FRIERS

144 John Rocque's map of 1746 records the medieval topography of the area around the Abbey. The Abbey Bridge led to the west front of the church and then passed into the Horse Fair, the Abbey's own market place. The walled gardens east of the church were where 'every Wednesday most of the town the Ladyes and Gentlemen walk', according to Celia Fiennes in 1698.

145 The Abbey as seen from Abbey Bridge in 1731. The large building on the right had probably been the abbey guest house. The bridge crossed a branch of the Rea Brook.

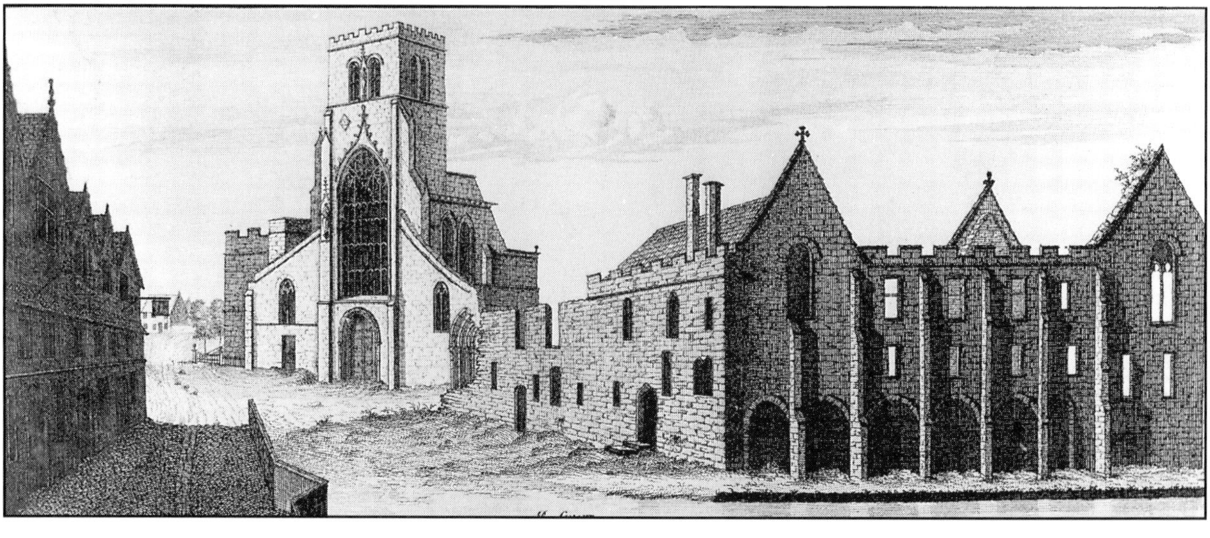

146 Travellers to and from Shrewsbury passed to the north of the Abbey until the present road was made in 1836. This painting of 1788 shows the patched up remains of the Norman nave and the 14th-century tower and north porch.

147 From the south, the Abbey took on the aspect of a rural ruin. It was set in a market garden locally famous for the strawberries and horseradish which it supplied to the parish. In this 1812 print the empty remains of the west cloister are occupied by poultry.

148 The road through the site of the Abbey cloisters was opened in 1836 by a procession of 15 coaches and two bands. Thomas Telford engineered the project as part of the Holyhead Road improvement. All but the west range of the cloister and the refectory pulpit had been demolished centuries earlier, but much archaeological information, which would have added to our knowledge of this important but poorly documented monastery, went unrecorded.

149 Work on the tower was in progress when this double funeral took place in October 1907. The two men, GPO clerks, had been killed in an horrific night-mail train crash just outside Shrewsbury station. Seventeen other people died in the accident which has never been fully explained. The disaster stunned local people, as can be judged by the crowds outside the Abbey.

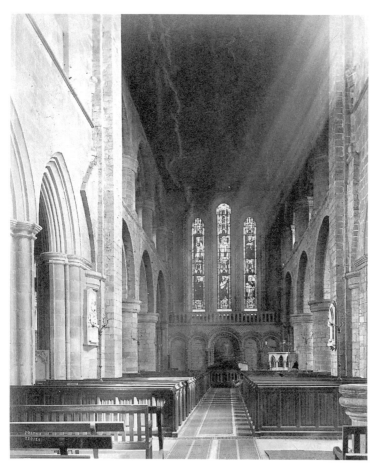

150 The nave of the church had served as a parish church for the people of Abbey Foregate in the Middle Ages, so was saved when the monastic part of the site was sold in 1540. This view shows the truncated building *c*.1880. The church had been restored to this state by the Shrewsbury architect S. Pountney Smith in 1862-3.

151 The grand scheme for rebuilding the eastern half of the church to cathedral scale, and possible use, drawn by J.L. Pearson in the 1880s had to be abandoned through lack of funds. However, his sympathetic new chancel of 1886 added dignity to a much-abused building.

38101. Shrewsbury Abbey Church Nave East. FF&Cº.

152 It is surprising that this 14th-century refectory pulpit was saved when everything around it was demolished. Artists and photographers were attracted to the Romantic Gothic ruin in the 18th and 19th centuries, but the relic's exposed position has long caused concern to those responsible for its preservation.

153 The domestic buildings of the Abbey included a water corn mill powered by the Rea Brook. It had caused a great deal of ill-feeling in the medieval period as the Abbot held the monopoly of milling for the town. By 1906 the mill had become a builder's store and timber yard. It caught fire and burned fiercely during an August night watched by an enthusiastic crowd.

154 and **155** These two photographs record a German prisoner-of-war camp set up during the 1914-8 war in the Midland Yard just south of the Abbey, which can just be seen through the trees growing alongside the Rea Brook.

156 Smiths at the Midland Railway-Carriage and Wagon Works, Coleham 1888. The works made railway carriages and tramcars from 1877-1912. In 1882 the first electric tramcars to be produced commercially were made here.

157 February 1946 produced another major flood seen here in Abbey Foregate.

158 Built in 1578-82, Whitehall was the grandest Elizabethan private residence in Shrewsbury. It was built by a lawyer, Richard Prince, using stone from the monastic part of the Abbey. As red sandstone is liable to deteriorate rapidly, the house was given a preservative coat of lime wash, which accounts for its name.

159 The coracle was for centuries the traditional craft for local fishermen on the Severn. This man, photographed in June 1892 in Whitehall Street, seems to have been hoping to catch salmon.

160 Shrewsbury Racecourse 1845, set out for the Royal Agricultural Show. The course grandstand built in 1839 to the design of Thomas Carline overlooks the scene.

161 This early aerial photograph, taken in November 1918, shows the extent of the Victorian and Edwardian Cherry Orchard estates. It also shows the extensive railway yards and sidings east of the station.

162 Foot traffic between Monkmoor and Uffington was once sufficient to justify a ferry. This view dates from *c*.1910 when Wilfred Owen and his family regularly came this way to attend services at Uffington church.

163 The Shrewsbury Canal, opened in 1797, ran through Uffington where a wharf and crane can be seen in this view of *c*.1930. On the horizon stands Haughmond Castle, a shooting lodge built *c*.1770.

164 Abbey Foregate, from its origins as a planned borough in the early Middle Ages, possessed an impressively wide thoroughfare quite unlike anything in the town centre. After a major fire in 1774 which destroyed most of the timber-framed houses, it was rebuilt with grand brick or stone-fronted houses such as Column Buildings on the left which were built by Thomas Carline.

165 As a focal point, Abbey Foregate acquired Lord Hill's Column in 1816. Hill's military achievements, combined with his personal concern for his men, caused him to be idolised by his contemporaries. A lodge at the base of the Column housed Lord Hill's trusted army acquaintance Serjeant Davies, who delighted in showing the Column to those prepared to tackle the 172 steps.

166 St Giles' church originated as the chapel of a 12th-century leper hospital established in rural isolation east of the Abbey Foregate suburb but near well-used approach roads which might be a source of alms. Until the 1830s the church was mainly used for burials, there being no parish cemetery at the Abbey. The Victorian development of the area resulted in the creation of a new parish of St Giles in 1851.

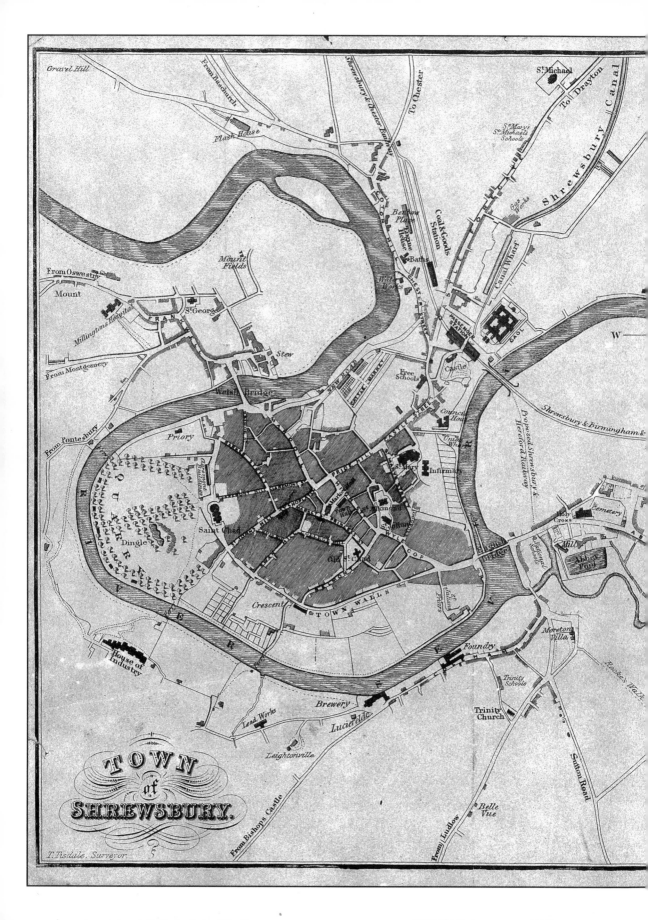

TOWN
of
SHREWSBURY.

T. Tisdale, Surveyor.